IMAGES OF ENGLAND

# AROUND TOTNES
## IN POSTCARDS

IMAGES OF ENGLAND

# AROUND TOTNES
## IN POSTCARDS

TOTNES IMAGE BANK AND
ROSEMARY DENSHAM

TEMPUS

*Frontispiece*: Totnes from the air. This 1920s photograph shows the jumble of ancient properties around the High Street of the old town. Towards the bottom of the picture, in the foreground, there is the C-shaped curve of the upper part of the main street called the Narrows. Then follows a glimpse of the colonnade which is the Butterwalk leading on to the handsome tower of the parish church of St Mary's. The roofs of the pannier market are visible halfway up on the right. Off to the lower left, but not in view, is the castle. Today the fields in the upper area of the view lie under the homes on Priory Drive, Avenue and Hill, Station Road and Colebrook Cottages. Just visible at the top is the track bed of the Quay Line railway branch and the river Dart. (Airco Aerials Ltd)

First published 2004

Tempus Publishing Limited
The Mill, Brimscombe Port,
Stroud, Gloucestershire, GL5 2QG
www.tempus-publishing.com

British Library Cataloguing in Publication Data.
A catalogue record for this book is available from the British Library.

ISBN 0 7524 3190 0

Typesetting and origination by Tempus Publishing Limited.
Printed in Great Britain by Midway Colour Print, Wiltshire.

# Contents

# Foreword

This is the second publication from the Totnes Image Bank. *Around Totnes*, now in its second edition, was the first compilation from the archive of our prints and negatives and photographs lent or donated by local people. These comprise part of the ever-growing digital database of local photography.

Rosemary Densham made available her collection of over 1,200 local postcards for the Image Bank to scan into the database. When this process was completed it became apparent that within this collection of postcards there was the material for a second book – *Around Totnes in Postcards*. This book is an excellent example of how the heritage of Totnes has benefited from such a collaboration. Private collector, Rosemary, and the Image Bank's organization and skills bring together a story of yesterday's images of old Totnes.

The Totnes Image Bank Trust's policy is to make available images of Totnes and the surrounding district. We achieve this through publications, exhibitions, a website, lectures, newsletters and of course the database, which by Spring 2004 will contain over 7,500 digital images. The Trust's income comes from the sale of books like this one, sales of high-quality photographic prints from the archive and database, and subscriptions to the Friends of the Totnes Image Bank.

Come and visit us in Totnes, or if you are far away keep in touch with our website and e-mail any enquiries or comments. Please let us know if you have photographs of Totnes that would be a valuable addition to the Image Bank's archive. You can donate or loan material for scanning with full credit given to the photographer and donor.

Barrington Weekes
Trustee and Project Manager

## Acknowledgements

Bill Bennett MBE, 1989. *The Totnes Collection*; Maureen Bridge & John Pegg (editors), 1998. *The Heart of Totnes*; Kelly's Directories, 1901 & 1923; Anthony R. Kingdom, 1977. *The Ashburton Branch (and The Totnes Quay Line)*; Vic Mitchell & Keith Smith, 2001. *Newton Abbot to Plymouth including Totnes Quay*; E.N. Masson Phillips, 1985. *An Industrial Archaeology Tour of Totnes*; Percy Russell, FSA, 1964. *The Good Town of Totnes*; Totnes Museum Society, 1981. *Totnes Remembered*; Totnes Museum Study Centre; Totnes Town Council. *Totnes Guildhall*; Whites *Devon – 1850 Directory*; Michael Young. *The Elmhirsts of Dartington*; H. Gordon Tidey, R.E. Toop, Cedric H.S. Owen, J.B. Sherlock, Peter W. Gray and H.C. Casserley: photographers of railway subjects.

Totnes Image Bank, Town Mill, Coronation Road, Totnes, Devon TQ9 5DF
Website: www.totnesimagebank.org.uk
Phone: 01803 862183

# Introduction

Picture postcards came into being in 1894 and quickly caught on with the public. Their attraction was the facility of being able to write a short message that would be delivered quickly and cheaply, with the bonus of a picture sometimes showing to family and friends where one was staying. The postal delivery service at that time was such that a card posted locally early in the day might easily reach its destination that evening, and certainly by first delivery next morning. The years between 1900 and 1914 are known among collectors as the 'golden age' of postcards. The onset of war in Europe coincided with the decline in postcard usage. Although there are many cards still about, which depict scenes from the Great War period that were sent home by the huge number of young men who went to fight in France and Belgium, their popularity waned. Earlier picture postcards had a wide margin where the sender could write a message. Post office regulations of the day required that the 'front' of a postcard should be used only for writing the address of the person to whom it was to be sent. The picture side was deemed to be the 'back', and that is where the picture and correspondence could appear. Such cards are known to collectors as 'undivided backs'. A few of these cards, with messages on the picture side, have been illustrated in this book. A few years later, the post office permitted the message and address to be written on the front, allowing the image to occupy the whole of the back. Nowadays, most people consider that the front is the side that carries the picture, with writing areas for both message and address on the back. Collectors call these cards 'divided backs'.

From the 1970s onwards came another golden age of postcards. This time it was for dealers and collectors who recognized the value of old postcards. There are today probably as many collectors of postcards as there once were of postage stamps. The attractions of collecting old postcards include interest in topographicals, works by certain artists like Quinton and Cynicus, and subjects and views by local publishers like W.R. Gay, Chapman & Son, N. Horne, E. Morison, and the big firms including Photochrom, Harvey Barton and Valentine. There are also interests in novelty and humorous cards, and in aspects of local, family, social and postal history. Topics include streets and buildings – perhaps now redeveloped; local personalities like MPs, clerics and mayors; school and society group photographs; dress styles; churches and memorials; transport, including motor vehicles and riverboats; and postal markings. Then there are the messages, which can give an insight into what people a hundred years ago wanted to say to each other. As with other antiques, the fascination in collecting old postcards is almost boundless, allowing for specialization in as many fields as desired by the collector. Collecting old postcards is more than indulging in nostalgia; they are image treasures and keeping them safely will help preserve in a small way our community's heritage.

The pictures in this book are taken mainly from postcards collected since the early 1980s. Too often our local heritage of pictures has been diminished when photographs of family, family businesses and social events have been discarded when the owners die, move away or a business changes hands. We have not knowingly or deliberately reproduced any images that are subject to intellectual property rights of others or without the owner's permission. In this second book of the series most of the images come from postcards issued before the First World War. The scope of this selection includes local villages and some towns with which Totnes had strong connections, such as Littlehempston, Staverton and Ashburton which used to be linked by rail. A small town with a long history, and a borough until 1974, Totnes has many facets. It was the only Devon town, of fifty-one historic town centres nationwide, listed in 1971 by the Council for British Archaeology. It has nearly 200 buildings rated as having architectural or historical interest. A great number of changes and redevelopments of Totnes have taken place between 1970 and 2000, especially near the river.

I am indebted to my friend Mike Vinten for researching the images in the chapter on railways. Mike, himself a railway man who started his apprenticeship in Swindon in 1955 and became Engineering Director of Wessex Trains, is a keen amateur photographer. He has photographed and videotaped steam locomotives and other interesting railway subjects for ten years and has had some of his work published in specialist books. Thanks also are due to my husband Phil, who assisted me with all the other text, local historian and writer Bob Mann for proofing, and Barrington Weekes and Val Price of the Totnes Image Bank for giving hours of valued guidance and technical advice.

Rosemary Densham

one

Around Totnes

*The Old Guildhall, Totnes.*

*Above:* Besides the East Gate, this is probably the most photographed subject in Totnes. Now stripped of ivy and with its slated front and roof replaced, the sixteenth-century former sexton's cottage and Guildhall are on the north side of St Mary's parish church, on Ramparts Walk. The ground floor of the gabled building was at one time the town prison. The women's cell was on the left behind the pillars between 1624 and 1887 and the prison administration rooms were on the right. Upstairs is the mayor's parlour, with two windows, where the civic gowns are kept. To the left is an entrance into St Mary's churchyard. Out of the picture to the right is the building which housed the boys' grammar school until 1887 when it was moved to the Mansion in Fore Street. After that, the building became the police station with prison cells. Today the building is the office of the town council.

*Opposite above:* The Guildhall Council Chamber, from a postcard used in 1925. Merchants obtained permission to set up a Guild, and in the thirteenth century its members numbered 120. The first Guildhall was at No. 8 High Street. A week before he died, King Edward VI gave permission for the Priory of St Mary building, vacated in 1536 during the Dissolution of the Monasteries, to be used as the Guildhall. The canopy over the mayor's place was installed in 1553. In 1646, Oliver Cromwell and Sir (later Lord) Thomas Fairfax made plans at the tables in the upper chamber, which is now used by the Town Council for its monthly meetings. Between 1624 and 1974 the lower chamber was used as a magistrates' court.

The Guildhall, The Council Chamber, Totnes.

*Right:* An attractive view of the old prison, adjoining the Guildhall, which was also the former sexton's cottage, from the lean-to covered entrance to the Guildhall. In 1895, the sexton's cottage was let to a Mr Eames for £4 per year plus the obligation to ring the 6 a.m. and 8 p.m. curfew bell and market bell. In the foreground are two of the granite pillars placed there in 1897, having been salvaged from the demolition of the Allottery (or Merchants' Exchange) which once stood in front of St Mary's church on the High Street. This postcard was postally used in 1955. (Jarrold & Sons Ltd)

*Above:* The interior of St Mary's church, showing the arrangement of the nave and chancel separated by its fine stone rood screen, which dates from 1450, and which was modelled on that in St Peter's Cathedral in Exeter. The tower is in the Perpendicular style. There are only ten parish churches in the county which have stone screens, and that of St Mary's is recognized as the most beautiful. Willis of London built the fine organ. (Nicholas Horne Ltd)

*Opposite above:* St Mary's parish church, seen before the memorial stones were removed. On the left are the backs of High Street properties and to the right (out of view) are the Ramparts Walk and the Guildhall.

*Opposite below:* Church Close is a narrow paved lane that runs northwards off the High Street between Nos 17 and 19, alongside St Mary's churchyard. It was widened when several houses were demolished, which stood where the railings are. At the time of this picture, Church Close provided access to North Street, the Guildhall and Ramparts Walk, the Church School, and Priory Avenue through a doorway.

East Gate viewed from the lower High Street. This postcard from around 1920 shows an old touring car driving downhill towards the 'Arch', which has been designated a Grade I listed building since 1952. No. 10, on the right, is a Grade II★ listed building, which retains structural features dating from around 1580. It stands on the site of a former mayor's house (William Ryder, 1432). No. 8, next down the road, was once the town's Guildhall.

The North Gate is the less imposing of the two gates remaining of the four that once served as entrances to the walled town. The road it spans was once the main route into town from Ashburton via Dartington, Barracks Hill and Malt Mill, before the major road-building programme introduced by the turnpike system. The simple stone archway, which has no passageway over, is seen here from the intersection with North Street on Castle Street. Once the property of Mr Francis Bingham Mildmay, a former MP for the Totnes constituency (later Baron Mildmay of Flete), this structure was given by him to the town. The entrance to the castle is along the pathway on the left. The card was postally used in 1905. (Stengel & Co.)

*Overleaf above:* The Butterwalk. From the fifteenth century on, 'the hose of fine Totnes' was sold here; the town was one of the main markets for cloth and clothing in England. In the next two centuries the trade turned to the sale of agricultural produce, and farmers set up their stalls here, before the pannier market came into being. This trade diminished in the mid-Victorian period. In several of these High Street properties there are fine carved plaster ceilings dating from the seventeenth century. This early postcard shows the first-floor rooms of these ancient properties upon the pillars, which were built at different times and are of different designs and materials. Some are constructed in crude stonework, some of dressed stone and arched, while others are of painted timber.

This later view shows, on the right, the overhanging properties of Poultry Walk, housing at No. 52, and the Lion Brewery of Messrs Walter & Phillips, brewers of Family Pale Ale, whose premises extended through to South Street. On the High Street there was, until 1885, the Lion Inn, later to become Boots the Chemists. At No. 50 there was Holman & Sons, seedsmen and general agricultural merchants, whose premises now house the elegant Quaker House tearoom. This Grade II listed building, mainly dating from the late eighteenth century, with its pillars on the street, has a fine stone open-hearth fireplace inside.

*Left:* A charming view of smartly dressed young girls posing patiently before the Victorian camera. This early card, with space for a message to the left, shows the High Street and upper Butterwalk and, opposite, the Poultry Walk on the right, seen from the Narrows. Note the horse-drawn carriage outside the newsagents at No. 56, which was then Taylor's, later Cuming's, and now Royberns.

*Below:* A later view of Butterwalk, looking down the High Street, with motor traffic. On the left is Reeve's furniture store and the Commercial Hotel is on the right.

Totnes, The Butterwalk

8460

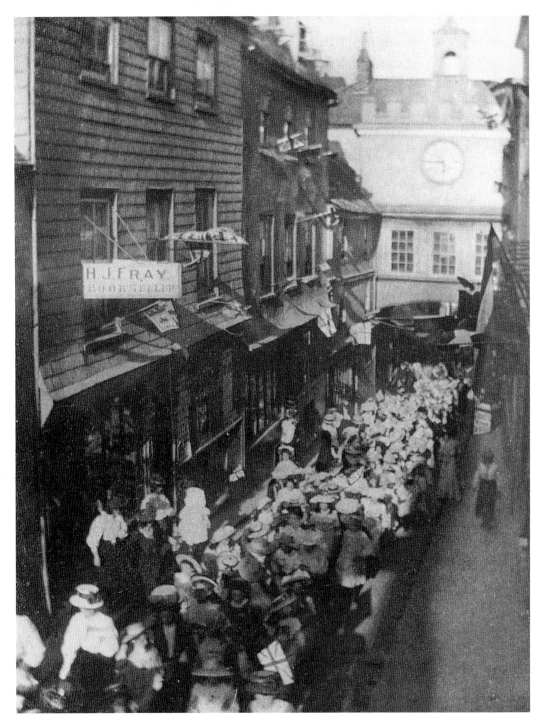

Patriotic parades in the High Street and Fore Street were a popular way to mark national occasions, especially Empire Day in May. Here an Empire Day procession is moving up the town and passing under the East Gate, around 1910. The shops closed for the day, and properties were decked with bunting and Union and colonial flags.

The Narrows in the upper High Street. The Plymouth Inn, at No. 97 High Street, on the junction with Collins Road, is on the left. The town's West Gate was located down the road, near the upper junction with South Street. The Gate was demolished in 1780 to widen this narrow, busy main street.

In the Domesday Book the Norman lord Iudhael (anglicized to Judhael in later writings) held the borough of Totnes (Totenais) from King William. The first castle is believed to have been built by Iudhael and to have been the seat of his barony. This view from the *baillie*, or outer enclosure, is of the castle which originated in the eleventh century. It shows also the access way up the man-made *motte*, or mound. The castle became the centre of Norman power for south Devon. It remained a stronghold until around 1485, when King Henry VII gave it to Sir Richard Edgcumbe of Cotehele. Today the wellbeing of the castle and its grounds is under the control of English Heritage. This real photograph postcard was postally used in 1965.

This interior view of the castle shows the arched entrance to the left and to the right the archway and steps leading to the shell-keep crenellations. The first castle, started in 1086, was originally timber-built and some 150 years later it was reconstructed in stone. It was positioned there not for defensive purposes, but to keep control over the surrounding populace. Castle bowmen, protected behind the merlons atop the wall, could target troublemakers without difficulty. Similar structures exist at Plympton and Barnstaple. This card was postally used in the 1950s. (Sweetman)

Up steep steps, you reach the single entrance gateway into the ancient castle. The semi-circular sandstone arch and the additional masonry reducing the width of the entrance are clearly shown. (Kingsway Real Photo)

A 1950s interior view of Haarer's Cruiser Cabin, Castle Hotel. This bar, fitted out with shipping paraphernalia, was named after Mr Haarer who ran the place in the mid-1930s. (Devon Commercial Photos, Plymouth)

A 1960s multi-view card which shows the Mount Plym Hotel, Plymouth Road, at centre, with clockwise views of the Steamer Quay, the Butterwalk, and also the dining room and lounge of the hotel. (Nicholas Horne Ltd)

The Plains area, seen here in 1904, is at the bottom of Fore Street, and to the west of and running parallel to the river Dart. In the centre is a monument, erected in 1864, in honour of William John Wills, born nearby in 1834. It was Wills, who with Robert O'Hara Burke, an Irish police inspector, and a party of eleven others, first set off to cross the Australian continent in 1860. They did it in four months, but perished from starvation on their return journey. The remains of these two intrepid leaders are buried in Parliament Square, Melbourne.

The Plains and Wills Monument. During the Second World War convenience overrode conservation. A concrete bus shelter was placed here in 1944, with buses coming and going around the Wills Monument. Fortunately, this unsightly shelter no longer exists, and the area was attractively redeveloped with pedestrians in mind and reopened in 1989.

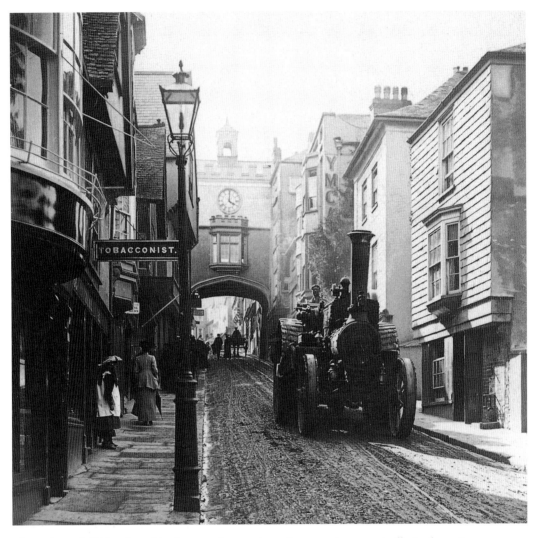

*Above:* Around 1900, when this photograph was taken, there was two-way traffic in the main street. The sight of a traction engine hauling a load of timber, perhaps towards the sawmills on the quay, was not uncommon. To obtain this shot, the photographer would have stood outside No. 58, then run by Mrs Martha Willis as a 'fancy repository'. Amongst other items, in 1902/03 she published and sold booklets of vignette pictorial postcards in sets of four (East Gate, North Gate, Fore Street and Castle). This must make her one of the earliest of the Totnes postcard publishers.

*Opposite below:* This uphill view of lower Fore Street shows, to the right, No. 17, which was then a newsagents and is now Phillips jewellers. Nearby is the former main post office and sorting office, built around 1925 on the sites of Nos 23 and 25 to replace premises at 1 Fore Street. It was difficult to build as the foundation trenches kept flooding. The gabled building was faced in brown Delabole slate in contrast to the larger traditional grey slates used further up the main street. In 1993, Royal Mail moved its sorting office to the Totnes Industrial Estate. In 2001, the post office moved again to the cramped interior of Local Plus, a convenience store, at No. 39. On the opposite side of the road is No. 22, an antique shop once run by William Harper, and No. 24, which in 1923 was run by Charles Smith, agent for Singer Sewing Machines. (Chapman, Dawlish)

*Above:* The King William IV Hotel is on the corner of Fore Street and Station Road. This rounded brick building replaced an earlier Elizabethan-style one demolished in 1902. Mrs Thomas Coombe ran the inn in 1901. Around 1900, an omnibus coach service to Paignton operated from the hotel three times daily in summer months, and twice daily in winter months. The road junction by the hotel (Station Road) was built in 1830 to enable traffic coming from Bridgetown to get to Ashburton without having to pass through the rest of the upper town.

This café, at No. 70 Fore Street, provided an old-world tearoom. This restored Elizabethan merchant house, with jettied front and high gable, and today the home of the Totnes Museum which opened in 1962, originates from the late sixteenth century. On conversion to a museum, the central entrance doorway was closed up and much wider windows on the ground and first floors improved the façade. The museum contains many exhibits of Totnes past and, on the top floor, there is a display on Totnes-born Charles Babbage (1791-1871), 'Father of the Computer'. It was Babbage who invented the 'difference engine', an early calculating machine.

In Edwardian days travel by pony and trap was common. Those on foot, not so fortunate, are seen here approaching the steeper part where Fore Street meets the High Street at the East Gate. This photograph taken in 1912 from just below No. 70 Fore Street, includes the house-decorating premises of Kinsman, later to become the Totnes Museum.

*Above:* Portland House, the columned porch and Regency façade of the Royal Seven Stars Hotel, the former post office at No. 1 Fore Street (the site is now occupied by Fulfords estate agents) and the rest of Fore Street up the hill. The 40-metre high pinnacled tower of St Mary's parish church breaks the skyline to the left.

*Opposite:* In 1723 Daniel Defoe stayed at the then Seven Stars Inn, built in 1660, which is conveniently situated at the north end of The Plains, where it joins lower Fore Street. This postcard view of the interior (probably by Chapman of Dawlish) shows the flagstoned foyer of the hotel. In the 1840s this area had been a coach entrance way. The staircase shown here leads to a dance hall/meeting room on the first floor. When the first cinema closed at the Seymour Hotel, it was moved here. Later the cinema moved to 27 Fore Street, now the shop of W.H. Smith. (Nicholas Horne Ltd)

*Above:* Fore Street, 1904. In the foreground on the right is the Totnes Quay Tramway entrance onto The Plains, alongside Portland House. This former tramway, initially broad gauge, ran from here to the Marsh Quay in 1873, and later became part of the Quay Line branch. Steam locomotives were not allowed to haul railway wagons on this section of the line, and horses were used instead at the time of this picture. Superior apartments were available in Portland House, and a Madame Chassant, teacher of languages, lived there in 1901. During its final years, it was named the Old Oak Café, a bed and breakfast establishment. In 1936, the building was demolished to make way for the construction of Coronation Road, opened the following year, which helped reduce traffic congestion in the lower Fore Street.

*Opposite:* Gas lamps hanging on the Wills Monument. On the left is the building of the former Wesleyan Methodist chapel, which became Symons' cider works. The buildings on the left were used as warehouses by Symons' and later by Graham Reeves Ltd, timber importers. The company for years was prevented from redeveloping this run down area. Permission was eventually granted for redevelopment into upmarket riverside residential apartments in 1989, and New Walk beyond, which has been extensively renovated and extended.

*Above:* Totnes Plains and lower Fore Street from Bridgetown and the river crossing, 1920s. There had been a tollgate (built 1826-28) spanning the highway in the foreground, erected to exact fees for crossing the river bridge. When the bridge had been paid for, around 1880, the two gates were sold off and publicly burnt. This was followed by a most jolly torch-light procession that went round the town. The limestone toll house, shown on the right, had a second storey added at a later date.

*Opposite:* Totnes Bridge. To obtain this view the photographer must have been positioned high above the entrance to the then Seymour Hotel. The picture captures a flock of sheep being driven over the river bridge from Totnes into Bridgetown, possibly destined for Luscombe's butchery at No. 4. This would have been a commonplace sight 100 years ago when there was a sheep market on Cistern Street, at the top of Totnes. This view takes in the former tollhouse, now a private house. Before the bridge was widened in 1692, a ford crossing a little distance downriver of the bridge was used at low water. (Harvey Barton & Son Ltd)

Since 1997, the old Town Mill building has been home to the Totnes Tourist Information Centre and more recently, upstairs, the Totnes Image Bank. The building, erected before 1588, was used for milling grist (corn) and malt and also in cloth-making. It is the last survivor of many such mills sited on a leat which discharges just upriver of the bridge, underneath the recently built Bridge Terrace. Originally the Town Mill had waterwheels on both sides, but in 1937, the defunct remains of the one on the town side were dismantled, and the wheel pit disappeared during the construction of Coronation Road.

The old mill and granary, with a cart bringing out goods from the mill. Both the old mill, with its broken waterwheel, and the adjacent large granary building, have been completely refurbished. The granary has become apartments and offices for the Safeway supermarket, with its large customer car park located behind. These properties are to be found on Coronation Road.

Warland, decorated for a coronation, probably of King George V in 1911. Similar leafy arches were erected in many small towns in south Devon on festive royal occasions. The photographer would have been standing near the present-day junction with Shute Road, and the view is towards the town. Some of the oldest houses in Totnes are to be found in this road.

This 1960s view of The Plains shows traffic being controlled by a white-coated traffic warden. Traffic wardens also controlled traffic at the Station Road junction in Fore Street and in the Narrows on the High Street. From this intersection of lower Fore Street with The Plains and Coronation Road, shown here, the main road ran eastwards out of Totnes over the Dart river bridge, through Bridgetown and towards Torbay. Today there is a mini-roundabout and Fore Street, now one-way, carries traffic away. Most vehicles are now able to bypass the town via the second (Brutus) bridge, opened in 1982, 200 metres upriver.

*Above:* The middle section of Fore Street, a busy shopping area. First on the left, at No. 38, is Hall's butchers shop and the pinnacle of the Methodist church. To the right are the attractive projecting upper windows in the Italian style façade of Lloyds Bank at Nos 31 and 33.

*Opposite below:* Dart Vale Manor, Bridgetown. This well proportioned nineteenth-century town house, which in recent years was a hotel, then a retirement home for the elderly, is again a private dwelling. Although it has lost some of its window mouldings during refurbishments, it retains its attractive Tuscan porch and quoins. (J.F. Lawrence)

*Above:* Totnes Grammar School, next to No. 34 Fore Street, on the left of what was for many years the offices of Mortimer Bros, printers and publishers of the local weekly newspaper *The Totnes Times*, started in 1860 (now Bradley's estate agents). The *Times* office moved across the road to No. 35 in 1971. Next up the street is the ivy-clad former grammar school, built as a town house around 1800. The brick façade once again became visible after Sir Alec Clifton-Taylor in a television programme on Totnes recommended authorities 'to get out the saws to remove the ivy'. This change was not deemed an improvement by all. The school for boys, founded in 1553 under charter by King Edward VI, was for some 350 years accommodated in a building adjoining the Guildhall, on Ramparts Walk. The school moved to the Mansion in 1887. Today the Mansion is used for exhibitions, adult education classes and other community activities.

Devon Terrace, Bridgetown, where the Exeter Road, now Newton Road, joins off to the right. Note the gas lamppost with fingerpost (to Newton and Exeter) on the left – the gas lamp has now gone and so has all the ivy. Next to the church of St John the Evangelist was a sub-post office and store business conducted from No. 10 Bridgetown (to the left of the church), which is now a residential dwelling. To the right is Devon Terrace, home of the author since 1978. At No. 8 Mrs Winifred Buckner ran a private school for many years after the Second World War, and in earlier times mayoral proclamations were made from that address. The houses in the terrace were built in pairs from about 1895 by Thomas Brooks, a builder trading at 33 Bridgetown. This postcard was postally used in 1908; the publisher is unknown. It is one of a series, three of which bear imprints FNA 784, 786 & 788.

A modern view of Bridgetown, showing large town houses built in the 1830s facing Devon Terrace. On the right is No. 17 Bridgetown, followed by the double-fronted No. 18 with Doric-columned entrance porch, known as Devonia in the 1960s. It became the Brymar Hotel, then a retirement home and now, known as Brymar House, is occupied by the Harris Dental Surgery. Next up the hill is Pomeroy House, which in Edwardian times was a ladies' college, an old people's home in the 1960s, and is now apartments, facing the junction with Newton (previously called Exeter) Road.

St John's church, Bridgetown. St John's church was built in the Perpendicular style in 1832. Referred to as St James in some records, it was a chapel-of-ease to Berry Pomeroy parish church. To the left is part of the Four Seasons guest house, previously Bridgetown Dairy & Grocery (Crooks). The postcard was postally used in 1947, and it was part of a numbered series by R.A. (Postcards) Ltd of London.

St John's church interior. Consecrated in 1888, the church was gutted by fire in 1976. Following rebuilding in 1980, meeting rooms, a ground floor foyer, toilets and a lift were installed. The east window was replaced with a bright sun design by Peter Tysoe, and provides an impressive focal point. It is now a multi-purpose building of greatly enhanced value to its congregation and the local community.

Lower Bridgetown immediately after the river crossing from The Plains. Bridgetown, which was a separate borough from the thirteenth century until incorporated with Totnes in 1832, has many interesting old houses – many of those shown here have changed little since this Edwardian view. In fact the only notable change in about 100 years is the absence today of metal railings which fronted these town houses. They disappeared in scrap-metal drives during the Second World War.

Seymour Terrace, Bridgetown. This stucco terrace of six houses, built around 1830, is on the left side of the main thoroughfare. Uphill from the terrace comes Harlyn at No. 36, which in 1901 was the Bridge Inn. Many years later and until the 1990s it was a guest house. Next up the street is a pottery, followed by seventeenth-century cottages, which still stand but have been much modernized.

two

# In the Town

The Queen Victoria memorial fountain, erected by public subscription to commemorate her Diamond Jubilee in 1897, is built of granite and Portland stone. It was originally prominently sited at the main entrance to the Borough Park on Station Road. With the increase in traffic, the memorial became a hazard and was dismantled and re-erected in the paved forecourt of the Dartmouth Inn on The Plains. It bears a plate indicating its renewed existence during the mayoralty of Mrs Valerie Austin JP, in 1988.

The Jubilee Fountain provided a drinking trough for horses at the approach to Totnes railway station. The structure shown here, quite hard to see, is bedecked with festive bunting. This marked the 1914 Devon County Show held at Totnes Borough Park nearby. This was the fourth time that the agricultural show had been held in the borough. In those days the annual show visited market towns before a permanent showground site was acquired near Exeter.

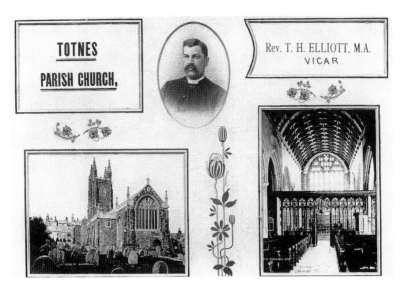

This early real photographic postcard shows St Mary's parish and priory church viewed from the south east, and the interior with its fine stone screen, silhouetted against the east window. Most of the memorial stones in the churchyard have been removed. Inset is a portrait of the then vicar, the Revd Thomas H. Elliott MA of Trinity College, Dublin, appointed in 1893, who was vicar for eighteen years. It was Revd Elliott who arranged for Messrs Hems & Sons, ecclesiastical sculptors of Exeter, to erect a tablet bearing the names of the past vicars of the parish, starting with Walter in 1260. The card was postally used in 1906.

General Sir William Riddell Birdwood. Lord Kitchener visited Gallipoli and Russell's Top, and is shown here with General Birdwood in November 1915. After suffering reverses, Kitchener supported evacuation of forces from Suvla and Anzac, which later took place in January 1916. The Gallipoli campaign against Turkey was a costly failure. 120,000 British Empire and 27,000 French troops became casualties. Of the 7,500 New Zealand casualties, there were 2,721 dead – one in four of those who had landed. Australia's 26,000 casualties included 8,000 fatalities.

GENERALS OF THE BRITISH ARMY.     *Portraits by Francis Dodd.*

### General SIR W. R. BIRDWOOD,
**K.C.B., K.C.S.I., K.C.M.G., C.I.E., D.S.O.,**

the Commander of the Australian and New Zealand troops who heroically made good their footing in the Dardanelles under the most desperate conditions ; and later won many striking victories on the Somme.

TOTNES CONSTITUENCY.

## Parliamentary Election
## 1929.

# HOW TO VOTE—

*(See other side)*

# WHEN TO VOTE:

The Polling Day is

## Thursday, May 30th.

Poll Open 8 a.m. to 8 p.m.

Major S. E. HARVEY.

The Conservative and Unionist Candidate.

**VOTE EARLY PLEASE.**

# WHERE TO VOTE ON MAY 30th.

YOUR POLLING PLACE IS AT

## Room No. 4, Wolborough Church School,
## NEWTON ABBOT.

Your Number on **RR 6124**     (P.T.O.)

*Left:* General Sir William R. Birdwood, CB, GCSI, GCMG, GCVO, CIE, DSO, LLD, DCL, DLitt, MA (1865-1951) was later to become a field marshal and styled Baron Birdwood of ANZAC and Totnes. He was born in Kirkee, India, in 1865. Rated one of the most heroic and effective generals of the British Army in the First World War, he had served on Kitchener's staff, and in 1914 was appointed to command ANZAC. He commanded the force at Gallipoli. When later it moved to the Western Front, this unit was reorganized as two corps. 'Birdie' commanded 1 ANZAC (later the Australian Corps) on the Somme, most notably during the struggle for Pozières. In September 1916, he became formal administrative commander of the Australian Imperial Force. He was knighted in 1916. In May 1918, he was appointed to command the reconstituted Fifth Army, being replaced in the Australian Corps by Monash. In 1925, he was promoted to Commander-in-Chief, India. In August 1919, he was granted the Freedom of the Borough of Totnes. His family had been connected with Totnes for centuries, several of his ancestors having been freemen of the borough. The family name is found in Birdwood Court adjacent to the Civic Hall (which was opened in 1962), and in Birdwood House at No.44 High Street, formerly the Commercial Inn. (From a portrait series by Francis Dodd)

*Above:* This aerial view of the old town clearly shows the oval layout of the walled Saxon/Norman settlement. Although little remains of the town walls, the individual property borders once defined have mostly retained their positions to this day. In the foreground is the curve of South Street, next comes the straight line of the High Street and beyond that the curve of North Street. Prominent features are the parish church of St Mary's and the market area. Priory Avenue, Priory Gardens and Priory Court were not yet built. (Surrey Flying Services Series)

*Opposite below:* This is a privately printed card notifying a registered number (RR6124) to a known supporter of Major Samuel E. Harvey (born 1885), who was the successful candidate in the Totnes constituency for the Conservative and Unionist Party in the parliamentary election of 30 May 1929. On the reverse of this card appear the names of the two other candidates, Messrs Rowsell and Spurrell. In fact Sir Samuel, as he became, was Totnes MP for the periods 1922-23 and 1924-35. He was knighted upon his retirement in 1935. His illustrious father, Sir Robert Harvey (1847-1930), who had studied engineering and worked in Bolivia, Chile and Peru, was chairman of several railway and waterworks companies, Deputy Lieutenant of Devon, High Sheriff of Devon and of Cornwall, knighted in 1901, resided at Dundridge House. (Mid-Devon Newspaper Co., Newton Abbot)

This stereo card, by an unknown publisher, depicts lower Fore Street. It shows the townspeople smartly dressed, and flags flying, on a fine summer's day. At least two flags have an ostrich in their design. The photograph is thought to date from around 1895. It is not known what is being commemorated.

Most postcard collections include stereo cards. When looked at through a special viewer, these double photographic images acquired depth, or a three-dimensional effect. Such cards were obtained by using a special camera having two lenses spaced about 10mm apart. The cameras and special viewers were made between 1850 and 1900. This photograph was taken around 1870 and this view of lower Bridgetown is little changed. However, No. 36 Harlyn, seen here as Farley's Bridge Inn, is no longer a public house and has had its façade rebuilt in Victorian terrace style. (Devonshire Illustrated, by Francis Bedford, #1979)

The borough regalia include two maces, a mayor's chain and badge and mayoral seals. The maces of silver gilt are believed to have been presented to the town by Sir Richard Lloyd, MP for Totnes from 1754 to 1759. The mayor's chain and badge, provided by public subscription, were presented to the Totnes Corporation in 1875; the gold chain is 104cm in length. The council also possesses a silver loving cup, 23cm in height, which is said to have been presented by Sir Edward Giles, MP for Totnes in 1620/21. The message written on this card in the hand of Edward Windeatt, Mayor of Totnes for his second term, sent to a Walter M. Hitchcock Esq., reads … 'Heckwood Totnes, 28 Dec 1912. Very many thanks for your beautiful and interesting book 'Reminiscences Volunteer Fireman', which I shall value. Also thanks for congratulations on mayoralty. Edward Windeatt, Mayor of Totnes, Devon.' Edward Windeatt (1846-1921), a solicitor and author, served the town well for twenty-three years as Town Clerk, then four times as Town Mayor. (Brock, Totnes)

The imposing northern elevation of Broomborough Hospital, on Plymouth Road, 1900s. On the roadside of the Poor Law Institution (Totnes workhouse) site, which had been built in 1838/39, was added a new two-storey red-brick and Portland stone infirmary. It opened in 1909, providing eighty beds. After the Second World War, the hospital was taken over by the newly created NHS. The last baby to be born there was in 1978. In its final years, it was used to treat geriatric patients. On closure, in 1993, the thirty patients remaining were transferred to a newly built community hospital on Coronation Road. The brick building was demolished and the whole area has been redeveloped into residential properties. The stone-built former workhouse at the rear, a listed building, has been transformed into residential apartments, and an impressive new apartment building put up on the roadside.

A ward in Broomborough Hospital in the 1930s, with patients of all ages posing for the picture. In front of the matron and nursing staff is a nativity scene set out on the table, with three pyramids, three wise men just visible, some palm trees, and in the corner a manger. Other than the tableau and a paper lantern decoration (top right), it does not appear like present-day hospitals at Christmastide.

The purpose-built hospital on Bridgetown Hill had its own rear garden for the supply of vegetables to patients and staff. The Totnes cottage hospital, built in 1900, took the place of the one run for six years at the leased property Algoa Villa, now the Smugglers Inn, on Steamer Quay Road. The cottage hospital served the community for about 100 years, and following the building of a new, larger hospital on Coronation Road, the old property was demolished and the site was used for the residential development at Varian Close.

The Priory, an elegant seventeenth-century stone mansion in its own grounds, at the end of Priory Drive, in the 1960s. It lies between the Ramparts Walk and Malt Mill (Jordan's) Brook. In the garden there is a cellar with running water. (Nicholas Horne)

| POSTCARD TELEGRAM | | *copyright* |
|---|---|---|
| To } JOHN. | | |
| Return Address } | From: DADDY. | |
| Arrived | last June. | |
| Weather | Raw. | |
| Scenery | Gorgeous. | |
| Drives | Numerous. | |
| Walks | Still more so! | |
| Boating | Up & down the DART. | |
| Amusements | Endless. | |
| Health | Perfect. | |
| Returning | NEVER !! | |

East Gate, 1920. The designers of this postcard, called a 'Postcard Telegram', had a bit of fun: a writer with little time or fondness for chit-chat was invited to note on it one-word responses to the questions set. Shown here is No. 14 High Street which was Jordan's, poulterer and dairyman. Next on the right is the South Devon Library. This card was postally used in December 1920. (G.W. Taylor, Totnes)

| POSTCARD TELEGRAM | | *copyright* |
|---|---|---|
| To } | | |
| Return Address } | From: | |
| Arrived | | |
| Weather | | |
| Scenery | | |
| Drives | | |
| Walks | | |
| Boating | | |
| Amusements | | |
| Health | | |
| Returning | | |

Another card in the Postcard Telegram series depicting the Butterwalk as seen from the Narrows. Taylor's the newsagent, at No. 58, is on the right with the Poultry Walk. (G.W. Taylor, Totnes)

Daw's Creamery novelty card. This diminutive silver-coloured milk carton card contained within it a pull-out strip of twelve views of Totnes. Having no place for the name and address, a separate label was attached for addressing purposes and a 1d postage stamp affixed, which is postmarked 1917. This type of memento was on sale in other towns having a dairy cream connection, with the appropriate town name overprinted. Daw's Creamery milk factory alongside the railway station was part of Cow & Gate, later Unigate, and now Dairy Crest.

A postcard drawn by one of the best-known and best-loved humorous Edwardian postcard cartoonists, the Scotsman Martin Anderson (1854-1932), who signed himself Cynicus. The names of tourist towns all over the country appear overprinted on these jolly, colourful and intricate drawings by the artist. Here we see *The Flyer* steam train struggling to get from Totnes to nearby Staverton (presumably a fore-runner of the popular Dart Valley Railway), with some staff dozing, some reading newspapers or others getting in a bit of cricket. This card was postally used in 1907. (Cynicus Publishing Co. Ltd)

An attractively composed Art Deco-style collage on a postcard. Inset are better-known Totnes town views of the river bridge, High Street, lower Fore Street, North Gate, Fore Street and St Mary's parish church. (N. Adams, stationer, Totnes)

three

# Work and Play

Outings by charabanc were very popular with both locals and visitors to the area after the First World War. Here an eighteen-seater Grey Cars Lancia is about to set off for a circular trip taking in Dartmouth and Totnes, according to the sign on the running board. Before departure, it was the practice for passengers to pose for a group photograph, so they could take home copies as a holiday souvenir. The charabancs operated from Paignton, and these sturdy vehicles provided excursions along the hilly roads of Dartmoor, among other trips. (Vickery Bros, Paignton & Exmouth)

Two new single-decker Western National buses, HOD65 and HOD66, which operated between Dartmouth and Totnes including the villages on the way. No location is evident from this picture but it may well have been in the vicinity of the large former Western National garage on Ticklemore Street, now converted to housing and residents' car parking.

Totnes Carnival was always an occasion to let your hair down, poke fun at authority and be topical. This photograph, probably pre-Second World War, taken on The Plains, shows slogans and posters referring to issues of the day: New Town Hall, Hanging of the Rate Collector, Free Air Passage over the Narrows, The New By-Pass Road. Clearly a few swipes are being taken at the town council. The man with the Cyrano nose, front left, appears to be adorned in a makeshift mayoral chain! The ladies in disguise at the back include Mrs Goodrich, Mrs Covin and Mrs Massey.

A hunt meet on The Plains, with riders and hounds. From the diminished light, this is probably the return of the huntsmen via Bridgetown. The leafless tree in the picture suggests it is wintertime. Boxing Day was a traditional date for fox hunting. Centre stage is the photographer with his camera tripod ready to record the scene. The card was postally used in December 1908, and the writer says *'You will see someone you know in the foreground'*. Perhaps the writer was the gent in the bowler.

The hunt has assembled and has acquired an encircling crowd of spectators. To the left are the bow-fronted windows of Portland House, the tramway gate, Henley & Sons cider store (later Harrison's Garage) and the Tollhouse. The card was postally used in June 1908, and the writer (not the same person as above) says *'I am in the crowd'*.

The hunt at the Royal Seven Stars Hotel, 1908. The stirrup cup tots are being dispensed to the huntsmen assembling at the meet on The Plains. (W.R. Gay's series)

Fairseat Club and the hunt, ready to set off. This building, to be found not far from Steamer Quay, has an interesting history. A private house called Algoa Villa was acquired initially for three years for conversion into the Totnes cottage hospital and support in cash and kind was solicited by the specially formed committee to finance and furnish the new hospital. It officially opened for patients in October 1885, with the Duke of Somerset as patron. It was succeeded by a new purpose-built hospital at Coldharbour on Bridgetown Hill, which opened in May 1901. The building later housed the Fairseat Club, shown here, until the Second World War when it was used as the main offices of Frank Curtis Ltd, wartime shipbuilders. It is today the Smugglers' Inn, a commodious and well-patronized pub and restaurant.

The mayoral party leaves the Seven Stars Hotel after luncheon on Empire Day. The period between the Boer War and the First World War was a time of raised nationalism. There was competition for status among several European nations leading to militarism and patriotic fervour. Lord Meath recommended that the nation recognize a new date in the calendar styled Empire Day. The day was the anniversary of Queen Victoria's birthday: 24 May. The mayor and corporation of the borough strongly supported this idea. Shops agreed to close, the town was dressed overall with bunting, and with the Union flag and the flags of major colonies. During the day there was a speech given by the mayor to the townsfolk who crowded The Plains area. The National Anthem and patriotic songs were sung. Telegrams expressing loyal greetings were exchanged between the mayor and King Edward VII and the Duke of Somerset. This postcard was postally used September 1909, and the writer asked '*Look out for father. Can you find him on the other side of the card?*'

*Opposite above:* The Plains was traditionally the place where townspeople gathered to mark coronations and Empire Day. This view is probably of the crowds assembled to hear the mayor's pronouncement about the accession of King George V (1910). In the background is Portland House, then the several riverside properties which were at that time mainly cider warehouses. The people on the right are standing on the route of the Quay Line tramway.

*Opposite below:* A parade of Boy Scouts. Besides the uniformed Totnes Volunteers, the town band, fire brigade and police, there were also young boys' organizations and school groups that paraded prominently on royal occasions.

Empire Day 1908 was held on the Saturday before the old Queen's birthday – 23 May. Standing on a carriage on The Plains, the borough mayor, Alderman Edward Windeatt, is addressing the people of Totnes. In his speech he referred to the fact that the Empire covered one-fifth of the land surface, and embraced one-fifth of the world's people. He gave loyal greeting to HM King Edward – The Peacemaker.

One of the patriotic songs the crowd sang illustrates their feelings: *Flag of Britain, proudly waving / Over many distant seas, / Flag of Britain, boldly braving / Blinding fog and adverse breeze / We salute thee, and we pray – / Bless, O God, our land today.*

The Plains, Empire Day, 1908. After the mayor's loyal address on Empire Day, townspeople processed from The Plains up the main street, led by the town band. There were field sports for the schoolchildren: running races, egg and spoon races, followed by a superb tea for 700 children arranged by High Street confectioner and baker George Cann.

These casual soldiers in front of the Seven Stars and Portland House are thought to be men of the Totnes Volunteers, pictured shortly before departure to battle in France during the First World War.

*Above:* Seen here in 1910 at their cookhouse are men of the 7th Volunteer Battalion of the Devonshire Regiment, who were camping at Totnes. There had been voluntary army companies in Devon since 1685, when defence against possible invasion from France was found necessary. (Charles Ricards, Totnes)

*Above:* The bacon factory built in 1912 by C. & T. Harris (Calne) Ltd provided much employment in Totnes for many decades. This scarce real photographic postcard shows the buildings just inside the main entrance by the Town Mill, with a modern brick built office beyond the covered steps. Seen here are the staff posing for the camera. The author had the good fortune to record, in March 1997, the memories of Mr Joe Seaford of Colebrook Cottages, who had worked there. He recalled fashioning sewing needles from wood taken from a nearby box tree, to stitch up sides of bacon in hessian bags, and stack them on a lorry for delivery to Cornwall. He understood that the cottages were built around 1893/94 by 'Neighbour' Cole, for the mill workers who had to live nearby to maintain the turbine and other machinery. The card was postally used in 1914.

*Opposite below:* Totnes Company of the 5th (Hay Tor) Volunteer Battalion, Devonshire Regiment, met regularly to drill and parade. These activities took place weekly in the Armoury/Drill Hall, in the Market House Inn, High Street, and on the Race Marsh. Their three objectives were the art of rifle shooting, proficiency in military tactics and preparedness to defend the country. It was in 1885 that Lord Clifford obtained royal approval of the use of the name Hay Tor Battalion for these men. In his lecture at the Coffee Tavern Hall, in 1888, on the origins and history of the Hay Tor volunteers, Lt Col. Amery concluded with the rousing poem: *The brave old men of Devonshire! / 'Tis worth the world to stand, / As Devon's sons on Devon's soil, / Though juniors of the band; / And tell Old England to her face, / If she is great in fame, / 'Twas good old hearts of Devon oak / That made her glorious name.* Today the spirit lives on in the Territorial Army.

Here staff of Broomborough Hospital pose in theatrical get-up, some as pierrots, after entertaining the patients in the early 1930s. For more information about the hospital and its connection with the Totnes Union workhouse founded on the site, see Chapter 2.

The Guildhall stocks in 1907. In earlier times convicted wrongdoers might find themselves confined here as targets for abuse or hurled rubbish. Behind the pillars is the present-day Guildhall, built on an ancient site, once the Benedictine Priory of St Mary, founded in 1088. The old elm pipe on the left is a remnant of the water conduit, first installed around 1700, which supplied clean water from Broomborough into the main street of the town.

Follaton House, like many other large country houses, served as a voluntary-aided war hospital during the First World War. The building designed by George Repton was erected in 1826 for George Stanley-Cary whose family had owned Torre Abbey, Torquay, in the seventeenth century. The house is in the neo-classical style with a four-columned portico. The property was sold after hospital service in 1918, finally coming into the possession of the present owners South Hams District Council in 1973/74. It became a Grade II listed building in 1952.

Holidaymakers at Follaton House. After service during the First World War as a military hospital, for a few years Follaton House, on the Plymouth road, provided holiday accommodation to members of the Co-operative Holidays Association based in Manchester. Here we see such a group posing in the grounds. The building later became the offices of the Totnes Rural District Council.

These young pupils of the grammar school, attired in starched Eton collars and with two of their schoolmasters, would have known the school song, the chorus of which runs: *Vivat, floreat, Totnesia! Crescat, floreat, Totnesia! In saecula permulta floreat Totnesia!*

The Church or National School was built in 1877 in North Street near the parish church, and enlarged in 1892. It accommodated 400 children in 1900, with an average attendance of sixty boys, sixty girls and sixty-six infants. In that year John Dobson Graf was master, Miss Emily A. Billing was mistress, and Miss S. Granger infants' mistress. On its closure, pupils were transferred to the Grove (founded 1865) and Bridgetown primary schools. The school premises were converted to residential dwellings in the late 1990s and named Old School Flats; in one of the playgrounds Wakefield Cottages were built.

King Edward VI Grammar School was founded in 1553 and before moving to Fore Street in 1887, as shown here, occupied a part of the Old Priory buildings (near the present day Guildhall). Famous old boys include Charles Babbage, father of the computer and one-time professor of mathematics (1828-1871) at Cambridge, and many others distinguished in theology, literature and science. Primarily a day school, the grammar school nevertheless had accommodation for thirty boarders. In May 1896, an old boys' society was formed with the mayor Thomas Creaser Kellock presiding at the inaugural meeting.

The attractive columned entrance porch to the Mansion at No. 36 Fore Street when it was the King Edward VI Grammar School. (Nicholas Horne)

# four

# On the Dart

*Above:* This upriver photograph, taken from below Steamer Quay landing stage, shows a paddler under way to Dartmouth. River Dart trips to Dartmouth are a major feature of holidays taken in Totnes. The tower of St Mary's parish church breaks the skyline. The postcard was postally used in 1959. (Valentine & Sons)

*Opposite above:* Steamer Quay jetty with the paddler *Kingswear Castle* alongside. The whistle is being blown announcing imminent departure downriver. This vessel was built by Phillips of Dartmouth in 1924, was disposed of in 1967 to the Paddle Steamer Preservation Society, Medway, and after refurbishment is still in use.

*Opposite below:* Taking on board passengers at Totnes landing stage, bound for Dartmouth.

To the right is the Island and to the left St Peter's Quay where merchant vessels brought in and took on cargoes. A sailing barge is seen here, but larger motor vessels brought timber to the quay in later years. The stone warehouses in the background were once part of the Symons' Cyder business and have been converted to housing. In earlier centuries huge volumes of goods were despatched and received here. Salt, coal and timber were imported, and tin, iron ore, stone, wool, potatoes, salted fish, corn, cider and copper were exported, the last by rail from Ashburton. The river trade in this place has a history stretching back to Norman times.

The Island, the bridge and the Steamer Quay wharves and warehouses. The sailing barge berthed alongside would have been involved in bringing in and taking out smaller cargoes.

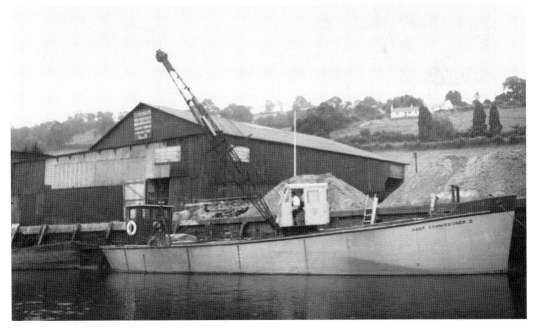

Commercial activities on the river comprised not only the import and export trade operated at Seymour Wharf (Steamer Quay) and St Peter's Quay on the Totnes side, but also sand extraction. Here, in 1953, a sand dredger is discharging alongside Sand Quay. The black sheds behind the crane jib were for storage of timber imported by F.J. Reeves Fox Elliot Ltd from Scandinavia.

*Above:* A 1940s wintry scene of St Peter's Quay with railway wagons at the far end of the Quay Line branch. The line had been constructed to handle imports of timber for Reeves and apples for Symons' Cyder and exports of cider. Vessels would moor alongside the Mill Tail quay for cargo handling. Trade had generally declined after the Civil War, aggravated by the disruption of foreign trade and high taxes. The arrival of railways all over the country in the nineteenth century caused the greatest reduction in water-borne commerce. In the case of the river at Totnes, only the imported timber trade was to survive into the 1990s. (C. Taylor)

*Above:* The stretch of water downriver from the Island has provided sport and spectacle to generations of Totnesians and visitors alike. Spectators in this very early view of Syms Brothers' boathouse urge on the boat crews competing in the upriver races of Totnes Regatta. The two-storey building to the left was the cider-making works of Symons' Cyder. That building was demolished many years ago; the cleared area formed the open storage area of Sand Quay. Today the new offices of Tor Housing occupy the site.

*Opposite below:* A 1903 view of the Steamer Quay landing stage. The tall smoke stack on the paddler indicates its early origin. Due to the increasing cost of coal, paddle steamers were phased out in the mid-1960s. This New Year greeting card was postally used in 1909.

The Seymour Hotel, now apartments styled Seymour Court, is on the eastern end of the bridge, overlooking the river and the Island. In this 1950s scene people are enjoying afternoon tea on the garden terrace. In its advertising of that time, the hotel offered boating, golf, riding, rambling and tennis. The hotel was built by the 11th Duke of Somerset in the early nineteenth century. The double bow-fronted feature of the original hotel before extension reflects the design of Portland House on The Plains. This Grade II listed building has been converted into residential apartments and renamed Seymour Court.

The River Dart and Seymour Hotel at Seymour Wharf. This is the Bridgetown side of the river, just below the bridge, viewed from the downriver end of the Island.

The Seymour Hotel and Riverside Café as seen from the Island. The hotel has its own jetty for guests arriving and departing by boat. Before the Second World War it was owned by the River Dart Steamboat Company Ltd.

The stone warehouses on the east bank of the river were used for the storage of imports – coal, culm (cheap coal for firing limekilns), apples and other goods. They were demolished one by one over the years until the last remaining one housed the Totnes Motor Museum. In turn, that building was demolished in recent times to make way for riverside homes overlooking Vire Island. Here a pleasure boat is waiting alongside to take day-trippers to Dartmouth, which is about 15km down river from Totnes.

SHARPHAM WOODS.

*Above:* Part way between Totnes and Dartmouth is the village of Dittisham, seen here from Greenway. A would-be passenger could hail the small ferryboat by ringing the bell to arouse the boatman on the other side of the river. Greenway ferry is near the estate once occupied by Agatha Christie. Also in view is a Totnes-bound paddle steamer.

*Opposite above:* A 'fish pass' was constructed in 1895 on the Totnes weir, near the railway bridge over the river. In that year salmon sold for 1s 9d per pound. Today we would call the pass a salmon leap. The river once abounded in salmon and trout, and rod fishing was a major pastime near the weir. There has been a big reduction in fish numbers, probably due in part to a century of discharges from upriver factories, water treatment works and chemical run-off from farmland. (Valentine)

*Opposite below:* This dramatic photograph shows a paddler near Sharpham making for Dartmouth. The tall funnel on this vessel identifies this as an early photograph. In later years, the funnel height on paddlers was to become much shorter, as is seen in other pictures in this chapter. The card was postally used in 1915. (W.R. Gay's Art Series)

*Above:* Boats moored at the quay on Stoke Gabriel creek. This view of the River Dart shows the oak trees, from which the river's name is derived, growing down to the water's edge.

*Opposite above:* After the Second World War, the Western Lady shipping company operated pleasure boat trips up the river to Totnes from Torquay. This multi-view advertising postcard shows inset views of Dittisham and the Royal Naval College at Dartmouth, being two of the places that were visited. (Dearden & Wade)

*Opposite below:* Besides the larger paddle steamers which made trips between Dartmouth and Totnes, there were smaller craft providing outings for holidaymakers. Here one such boat *Black Swan*, facing upriver with the Island in the background, finds itself amidst a gathering of swans and gulls.

RIVERSIDE COTTAGES, DITTISHAM

THE PIER, DITTISHAM

WESTERN LADY

**WESTERN LADY**
RIVER DART CRUISE

DITTISHAM VILLAGE

DARTMOUTH & ROYAL NAVAL COLLEGE

RIVER DART TRIPS

*Above:* One of the pleasures of a summertime visit to Totnes was, and is, to take a river trip to Dartmouth, down the scenic river Dart. Here warmly-dressed visitors in 1927 queue on Steamer Quay for tickets to travel on one of the several paddle steamers operating the service.

*Opposite above:* Steamer Quay, 1925. This delightfully composed summertime view of the Steamer Quay jetty, seen from the shaded end of the Island, brings to mind the gentle pleasure to be gained from just sitting and watching the world go by. There is a paddler alongside the jetty. Because paddle steamers in those days had fixed drive shafts they could not set the paddle wheels to oppose one another in order to turn about. Instead the vessel's bows would be tied to the bank and the stern swung about to make the boat face downriver.

*Opposite below:* On a fine summer's afternoon, what could be more restful than a spot of leisurely fishing in the Mill Tail? Opposite is the town end of St Peter's Quay and in shadow the rear of Holman's store, built in the early nineteenth century as a town house. The Quay railway line ran on the other side of this building, in which Holman & Son conducted their seed and general merchants' business. Today, the refurbished stone building comprises attractive riverside apartments.

An upriver view from the bridge. The land to the left, now an industrial estate, was called Broad Marsh. From the late eighteenth century until the outbreak of war in 1939, this was where the annual Totnes Races steeplechase took place in September. Nicknamed the 'Ascot of the West', it was a major event in the horseracing calendar, on occasions drawing crowds of 50,000 spectators. Before the First World War, the 4-mile course extended from below what is now The Bourtons (former Chateau Bellevue site), around the quarry, along the Newton Road to Old Redhill quarry, then across the river (at low water) to the finish. On the east bank (Bridgetown side) of the river there was a ropewalk, where the long ropes used in sailing ships were made. The ropewalk consisted of parallel pairs of wooden pillars placed at regular intervals. It was roofed over its entire length and each pair of pillars had wide steel pulleys for weaving or 'laying' of the rope. In 1903, John Dawe Toope, living at 30 Bridgetown, was the rope and twine maker.

This general view north from Totnes Down Hill (the minor road to Ashprington) is recorded in a lithograph published by T. Hannaford some fifty years before picture postcards appeared. It shows the town of Totnes, the bridge over the river Dart and Bridgetown. On the skyline are the tors of Dartmoor. The river rises on Dartmoor and meanders via Totnes to Dartmouth and the sea. The Saxons established a *burh* (borough) here because the river was shallow enough to ford at low water and there was an elevated hillside to the west providing a defensive position. (Raphael Tuck & Sons Ltd)

Totnes regatta, 1933. The Dart Rowing Club has staged the Totnes & Bridgetown Royal Regattas for many years, usually in August. Seen here from the Island, two crews battle it out upriver, passing the Steamer Quay landing jetty with the clubhouse in the background. (F.C. Holwill, Dartmouth)

A post-war motor pleasure boat *Dartmouth Castle* with day-trippers setting off for Dartmouth. The river bridge appears in the background, and the Island to the left. (Raphael Tuck & Sons Ltd)

The river is tidal up to the weir; here it is flowing over Longmarsh at a time of very high water. Longmarsh, today a recreational area, was previously called Salt Marsh. Nearby are the remains of butts where soldiers practised rifle shooting before the First World War. The river is navigable for 22km up to the Totnes weir, and the tidal fall is just over 3m.

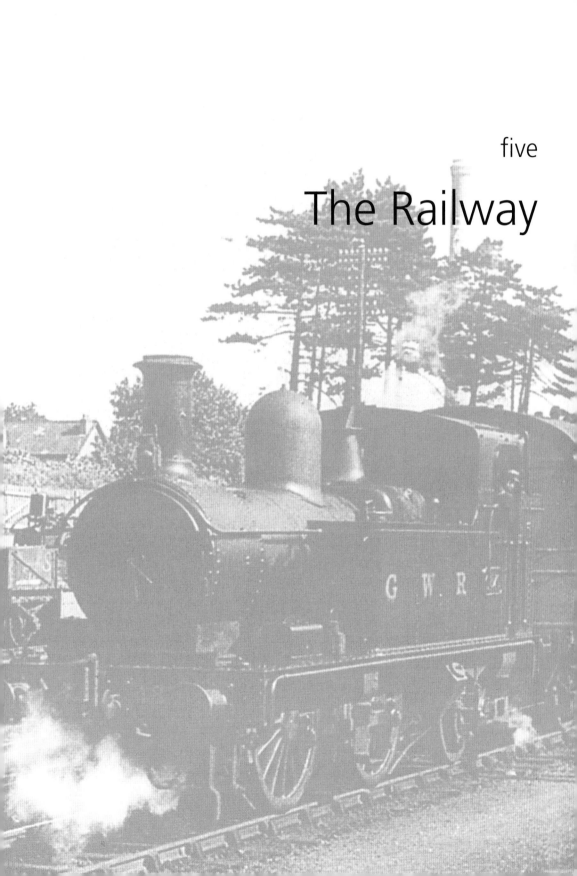

# five

# The Railway

*Above:* Totnes station, looking west from the road bridge through an old signal gantry at a well-wooded Follaton. This is the bottom of the Rattery bank – a long slog for westbound trains! New bracket signals, not yet in use, are visible near the water tank. The gradient is noticeable by comparing the main line with the level sidings on the right. The warehouses to the left were built in Regency times and are listed buildings. They have been unoccupied for many years. In 1901, William Hamlyn & Sons, coal merchants, and Joseph Roe & Co., wholesale grocers, had stores at the railway station to supply their shops in the main street of Totnes.

Totnes Station. This view focuses rather a lot on the railway lines as seen north-eastwards from the A385 road bridge. However, it is an early photograph and shows the Brunel atmospheric railway engine house and chimney, and covered areas alongside the up and down platforms. These timber roofing structures have long gone.

*Opposite below:* An Ashburton branch train at Totnes, 1913. It is headed by an early GW 517 class 0-4-2T No. 1466, built at Wolverhampton in 1883 and worked until 1935. At this time, the signal box was yet to be built. The Ashburton branch opened in 1872. This postcard was postally used in 1917. (E. Pouteau)

A Manor 4-6-0 7813 pilots a Castle Class on the up express through Totnes in the days before high-visibility vests had to be worn by anyone on the line and when station staff could use boarded crossings to cross the line. (H. Gordon Tidey)

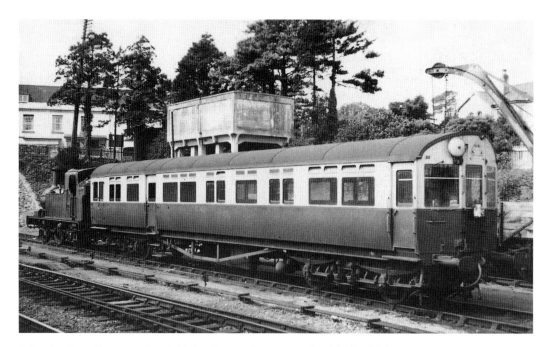

A local train at Totnes station. This is a later-style auto coach with the driving compartment coupled to a GW 0-4-2T. It has a 14NN number as did the old Wolverhampton locomotives, which had worked the line years earlier. The long-disused concrete water tower was dismantled in 2003.

Great Western Hall class 4-6-0 4950 *Patshull Hall*, unusually diverted onto the down platform track. Most trains needing to be passed by faster trains were 'looped' in the goods loops on the Newton Abbot side of the river bridge. To the right are livestock pens and a connecting spur line. (R.E. Toop)

Diesels arrived on British Rail around Totnes in the late 1950s. By 1964 steam locomotives had vanished. People started taking photographs of diesels; in this case a diesel electric Bo Bo class 24 is dropping down Rattery bank into Totnes, drawing a track-testing train seen here on 16 November 1976 from the western bypass bridge. St John's Terrace houses are on the left. (Cedric H.S. Owen)

*Above:* Station staff and crew against the backdrop of 3277 *Earl of Devon*, in a cloud of steam, at the down platform of Totnes station. The signboard informed passengers that they must change here for Ashburton. Upon reorganization, the Ashburton line was closed. The line, for most of its original route, is now privately run by the South Devon Railway from Totnes Riverside/Littlehempston, just north of the Totnes station river bridge. Visitors are able to enjoy a ride on the SDR steam trains via Staverton to Buckfastleigh in the summer months and on other special occasions. The route, known these days as the Primrose Line, passes through the scenic Dart valley, alongside the river for most of the way.

*Opposite above:* The Great Western Railway reached Totnes in 1847. The Dart Valley Railway's Great Western 2-6-2T 4555 and 0-4-2T 1466 are seen here on a special run in 1972. In the first coach were the dignitaries toasting continued success to the DVR.

*Opposite below:* Looking towards Ashburton junction and Newton Abbot from the station footbridge, showing the water tank for 'up' trains. The goods shed, which has an advertising panel for Van Houten's Coffee above, has a wagon-loading gauge. On the hillside beyond is the white building of Bourton Hall (later Chateau Bellevue hotel) on the Newton road. Enamelled trade advertising signs are attached to the platform fencing on the left. Beyond the goods shed the Quay Line branched off to the right.

A double engine at Totnes station on 18 September 1952, four years after nationalization. 5926 *Grotrian Hall*, with a Great Western liveried tender but a British Railways smoke-box number plate, pilots 6026 *King John*, in full British Railways livery on the 'down' Cornish Riviera. The pair are crossing Malt Mill bridge and about to do battle with the steep Rattery bank, just after passing Totnes station. (E.S. Rundl)

Totnes station after the Ashburton and Kingsbridge branches had closed. The name board used to read 'Change for Buckfastleigh and Ashburton'. A passenger for Kingsbridge would change at Brent. The 3,000-gallon glass-lined six-wheeled milk tanks carried fresh milk to London. Two milk trains ran through Totnes daily picking up at St Erth, Lostwithiel, Totnes and Tiverton Junction among others. Milk trains also ran up the Southern Railway route from north Devon to London. The lattice bridge was replaced after being struck by a crane jib, and the timber building beyond was replaced after a fire.

Totnes station from the downside platform with signal box, separate train sheds and the top of Brunel's engine house chimney just visible above the up platform roofing. Of interest here, between the tracks, is the point rodding, which connected the points to the signal box. This mechanical system was not as convenient as today's electric motor and cable, but the old system did not cause as many delays as modern equipment occasionally does! A goods train is disappearing towards Newton Abbot with an early Great Western goods guards van at the rear. The basic design remained in use until British Rail did away with most goods guards after all goods trains were fitted with continuous brakes. (The Locomotive Publishing Co. Ltd)

Great Western *Otterington Hall* 6983, a two–cylinder 4-6-0 double, heads a four-cylinder King on a down express, passing through Totnes under the GW footbridge, which was later damaged beyond repair by a track crane that could not quite pass under it.

*Above:* Goods engines at Totnes, 1960. Large and small Great Western Prairie 2-6-2Ts 4561 and 4555 appear to have just made use of the water crane, whilst running around a Sunday School special excursion from Buckfastleigh. The other locomotive is a large Prairie 2-6-2T used for banking freight trains up Dainton and Rattery banks. Redworth Terrace and the milk factory offices appear on the far side. (Peter W. Gray)

*Opposite above:* An early photograph of the station 'down' side approach road with signal box, station buildings, goods shed and Brunel's pumping house chimney. The pumping house, built in 1847, was a relic of a short-lived experiment for the original South Devon Railway that did away with the need for locomotives, propulsion being provided by atmospheric pressure. (J.B. Sherlock)

*Opposite below:* Great Western locomotives in preservation, 15 April 1979. 1450 (*Bulliver*) and 1638 pass the site of Totnes Riverside/Littlehempston station with an early Dart Valley Railway train.

A down express headed by a Great Western two-cylinder 4-6-0, with a good head of steam, dashes through Totnes middle road ready to tackle the formidable Rattery bank. The unusual wagon on the left is a gas tank. The gas was made by the railway to provide lighting and fuel for refreshment car cooking. (W.R. Gay's series)

Plymouth Railway Circle Ashburton special, 8 September 1962. Locomotive 4567 bears a special plate recording the event, hauling ten goods guard's vans laden with steam railway enthusiasts participating in the final run on the Totnes Quay line. To the right is the railway station, just visible; on the left is the present-day industrial estate and former racecourse. (Cedric H.S. Owen)

Ashburton branch train, Totnes, 30 August 1945. Daw's Creamery has its new chimney. Great Western 0-4-2T No.4870 with GW auto coach crosses from down to up main, ready for its next run. These old-style locomotives were built from 1932 to replace the ancient Wolverhampton-built 0-4-2Ts of 1883. Auto trains permitted the train to be driven from the cab within the coach to save running around on light branch trains. (H.C. Casserley)

Great Western 2-6-2T No.4567 with a Plymouth Railway Society special of goods train brake vans on 8 September 1962, marking the end of the Totnes Quay and Ashburton freight workings. The train is shown heading out of Totnes for Ashburton. This was the time when lines and services were being cut back, due mainly to under-funding of the railway system during and after the Second World War. (Cedric H.S. Owen)

Isambard K. Brunel, the famed Bristol engineer of the Great Western Railway, placed a pumping house at Totnes as part of the ill-fated atmospheric railway. Another such house is at Starcross. The building is seen here being used as a store by Symons' Cyder. Enamelled advertising signs for National Engines, Nestlés Milk and Camp Coffee are shown. The Creamery, a major employer in the town, now uses this building, which lies on the west side of the station.

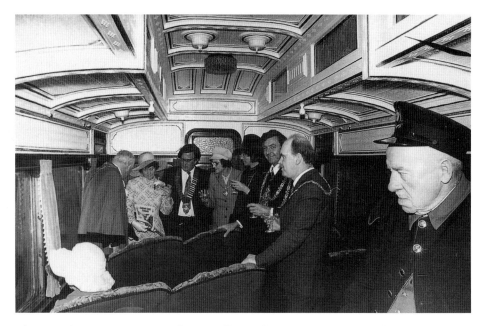

The Mayor's Carriage on a special Dart Valley Railway occasion, possibly the Centenarian train, illustrated elsewhere in this chapter. The coach is Queen Victoria's special saloon, the first vehicle on the Centenarian special. Totnes town sergeant Jim Maddock is shown in attendance.

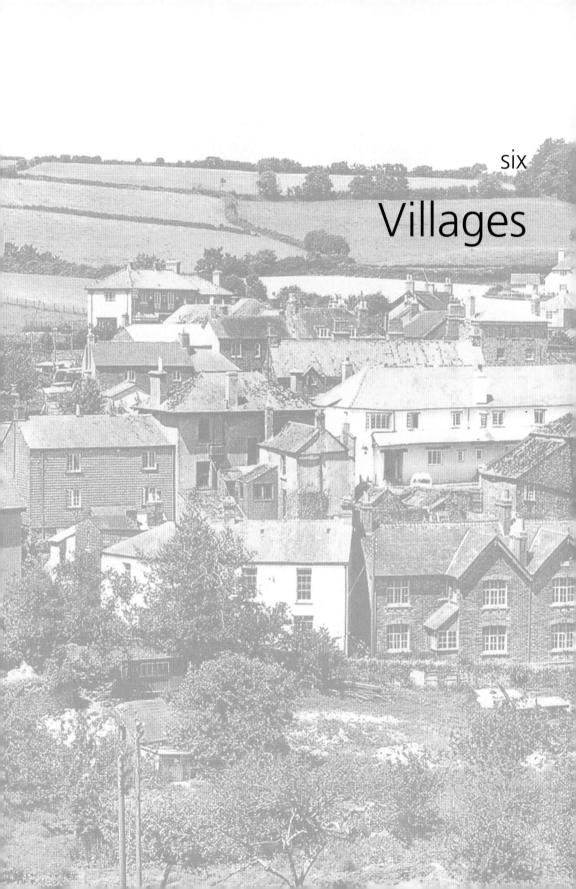

# six

# Villages

*Above:* A 1920s glimpse of the derelict entrance passage of Dartington Hall, adjacent to the Great Hall, before restoration. The hall, leading off to the right, is shown here open to the sky and the elements and the walls are clothed in ivy.

*Opposite:* This is the first view the visitor gets of the medieval courtyard of Dartington Hall. The site of this ancient habitation and village (Dertrintone in 1086) – first mentioned in a royal charter of 833 – is recorded as a baronial seat starting with the Norman Lord William of Falaise (1113), followed by the Tours, Fitz Martyn, Audley, Vere, Holand, and other families, then the Champernownes from 1560 to 1925. In 1850, Henry Champernowne owned two-thirds of the parish of Dartington. Some of these buildings are of great age and have been sensitively restored. Leonard Elmhirst (1893-1974) and his wife Dorothy acquired the estate in 1925. This dynamic and practical couple surrounded themselves with talented people to start up businesses, to foster employment in the depressed times of the 1920s, to introduce improved methods of farming and to provide modern education and culture. Visitors can enjoy strolling in the well-kept grounds and gardens, and realize what can be achieved by people who had, and still have, a vision of a better society. (E.A. Sweetman & Son Ltd)

Another view of the Great Hall, showing its fine arched windows and the wash of light which floods the interior. The hall is used for musical and other gatherings like the estate Christmas carol concert. Music stands are in place in the foreground. (Nicholas Horne)

The interior of the Great Hall after restoration in 1932, returned to its former stature with hammer-beams of oak from the estate, enhanced by fine modern banner tapestries. The eight tapestries, woven from wool by Elizabeth Peacock, contain designs to represent the main departments of the Dartington Hall estate.

The Lodge, Dartington.

Dartington Lodge, an attractive building off the Ashburton Road on the north-west edge of Totnes, at the entrance to the lower drive leading to the Dartington Hall estate, close to the Bidwell Brook. The horse and trap are heading towards the main road.

The former Lower Tweed Mill, built as an experiment, had handlooms, carding and spinning machines to make fine tweed textiles. It was erected in the mid-1920s, and is sited on the edge of the Dartington Hall estate near Shinners Bridge. Dartington produced top-quality woollen furnishing fabrics which were exported worldwide. The building is served by a leat with launder, running from a point a short distance upstream on the Bidwell Brook, which powers an overshot mill wheel. In recent times it housed a printing firm, since moved to Totnes, but is unoccupied at present. (Valentines)

Salmon Leap, Dartbridge, Buckfastleigh. No longer having a thatched roof and with a new name, the spacious Dartbridge Inn is a popular restaurant and pub near the junction of Ashburton Road and the Devon Expressway (A38) near Buckfastleigh. Well-known for its splendid roadside displays of spring and summer flowers, it is near the salmon leap on the river Dart. Across the river is the Buckfastleigh station of the South Devon Railway, the Butterfly Farm and other tourist attractions. This postcard was postally used in October 1950. (Kenneth Ruth)

*Opposite above:* The Queen's Arms on the Ashburton Road, between Puddavine and the Lower Tweed Mill, on the way to Shinners Bridge and the Cider Press Centre, Dartington.

*Opposite below:* The Cott Inn, on Cott Road in Dartington, about 2km west of Totnes. Note the date of AD 1320 painted on the wall of this ancient hostelry, which comprises a row of joined cottages with an attractive thatched roof. In 1989 the roof caught fire which caused huge damage. The building was renovated but retains an old-world ambience and, with its good restaurant and spacious bar, it is one of the more popular venues in the area. (Nicholas Horne)

*Above:* Another view of the Cott Inn, on the approach uphill from Shinners Bridge. This postcard was postally used in September 1957. (Nicholas Horne)

*Opposite above:* St Mary's Church, Dartington. The old parish church, next to the hall, was not conveniently placed and was pulled down. A new parish church of St Mary the Virgin, shown here, was built to the same design and used materials and five of the six bells salvaged from the old church. It was consecrated in 1880. It is located at the crossroads of the Ashburton Road and the road to Week, at the northern upper drive entrance to the Dartington Hall estate.

*Opposite below:* Staverton village (once Stouretona) is on the south side of the river Dart, about 5km north west of Totnes. To the north of the parish, about 3km south of Ashburton, are the old Penn Recca slate quarries, which produced roofing slate since 1338. Penn slate was used for roofing Dartington Hall. Later, after a period of disuse, a revival had a major influence on the development of the parish when Penn slate was used for the roof of the Houses of Parliament. At one time there were three pubs in the village, but only one remains today – the popular Sea Trout Inn, formerly the Church House Inn, which is near the middle of the village.

ST. MARY'S DARTINGTON.

Staverton

*Above:* Before the fourteenth century, people and packhorses had to cross the river Dart at a ford by Town Mills. The first bridge in the parish, originally about 2.25m wide, was widened in 1809. With recently added bollards at either end, motorists must use the bridge with caution. This excellent photographic view of the bridge and towards Dartington is seen from the railway station. The railway line to Ashburton, via Staverton, was opened on 1 May 1872. The branch closed to all traffic on 10 September 1962, the last BR passenger train having run in 1958. The Great Western Society restored the line and it was re-opened in 1968. (W.R. Gay's series)

*Opposite above:* Staverton's parish church of St Paul de Léon has a tower with a peal of six bells, recently restored at a cost of about £35,000. The wooden screen is not decorated and has a tall cornice. There is a font of stone, and columns of Beer stone. Vicars are recorded since 1148. In 1877, the church was restored in the usual Victorian manner.

*Opposite below:* A closer view of Staverton parish church. This is the third church to have been built on the site and dates from the early fourteenth century. In 1413, when the river bridge was in danger of collapse, the church financed its rebuilding by issuing Indulgences, a means of raising finance or labour in medieval times. Indulgences were sold to people so that they could spend less time in Purgatory – equivalent to paying a fine instead of going to prison. (Stengel & Co.)

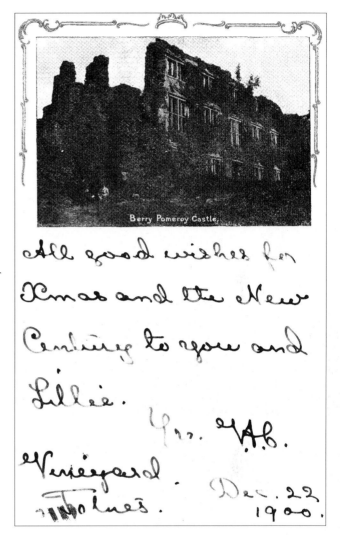

*Right:* This early undivided back postcard, postally used in December 1900, shows Berry Pomeroy Castle from below. The ruined castle is sited high on the eastern side of the valley and is impressive when viewed from the old mill. The village of Berry Pomeroy (Berie in 1086) is about 1km east of Totnes on the Paignton road. The parish comprises a mainly agricultural area of which the ruined castle, mostly dating from the fifteenth century, is a notable feature and tourist attraction. Shown here is the Elizabethan house, which was destroyed by fire and never rebuilt. Further decay has been arrested by English Heritage, which has reconstructed the chapel over the guardhouse. This is a place about which tales of the supernatural persist.

*Opposite above:* Fleet Mill, Totnes. Sometimes spelt Flute, the mill is a reminder of the importance of water power to milling in the Totnes area. The remaining gristmill building, which is thought to be one of two originally, has medieval origins, having jetties on the east bank of the river Dart, in the parish of Berry Pomeroy. It was first mentioned in records of 1378. A stone-lined leat leads to the building, the nearer section being capped in brick. The mill was used until the early part of the twentieth century. It is approached by a minor road from lower Longcombe, off the Paignton road.

*Opposite below:* Castle Mill, Berry Pomeroy. This postcard, postally used in July 1906, shows the old corn mill on the Gatcombe Brook, powered by an overshot waterwheel. In recent years the building was a souvenir shop, and is at the foot of the valley below Berry castle. It can be approached from the castle by walking down a steep meadow to the brook at the bottom, or by a minor road from nearby Afton. (Stengel & Co.)

This slate–hung toll house, erected by a turnpike trust, stood on the fork at True Street corner, where the road to Berry Pomeroy village leaves the Paignton Road just east of Bridgetown. Toll houses were erected under the turnpike system, and were the places where tolls were collected from travellers wishing to use a certain stretch of new or improved road. The word turnpike derives from the pike or barrier which was turned to allow access. The roads were maintained out of the toll revenue raised. The journey from Totnes to Torquay was expensive. In the eighteenth century a traveller was faced with two or three tolls when wishing to pass over Totnes bridge, up Bridgetown Hill, then from True Street onwards to Longcombe. The building shown here was a police house for a time but, after serious damage inflicted by a lorry, it was completely demolished in 1971.

Chateau Bellevue hotel, about 1km from Totnes on the Newton road. It was built as Bourton Hall and subsequently renamed, realistically but perhaps unimaginatively, Chateau Bellevue. This interior view shows the cellar bar during its time as a hotel, when it offered bridge and tennis, and had a swimming pool. The Chateau Bellevue is remembered with affection by the author as the place of her wedding reception in 1965. Despite a hope that the hotel building might have been interesting enough to be listed, it fell to the demolishers' hammers to make way for a cluster of well laid out residential homes called The Bourtons.

Ashburton is not a village but a very attractive old market town on the edge of Dartmoor. Ashburton is one of the four Stannary (tin industry) Towns. Since 1285, when it was so designated, until 1515 when it was most prominent, nearly 40 per cent of Devon's tin was sold through Ashburton. By the early eighteenth century this trade had all but finished. Today it is a quiet town, with a couple of main shopping streets, a town hall and a museum, very much like Totnes, with many properties having slate-hung façades. The town was once connected by branch railway line to Totnes. (Chapman, Dawlish)

The Old Church House Inn, Torbryan. The hamlet (once Torra, meaning a hill) is approached from Ipplepen or Broadhempston along narrow Devon roads. This mainly sixteenth-century coaching inn, with old-world charm, offers comfortable en-suite bedrooms, excellent food and real ales. Opposite is the lime-washed redundant parish church of the Holy Trinity, built around 1400 in the Perpendicular style. The church is under the care of the Churches Conservation Trust, set up in 1969, to care for Church of England churches no longer needed for parish use. All its churches are architecturally or historically important with most classed Grade I or Grade II★. There are over 325 churches so managed that are thus able still to extend a welcome to visitors.

*Above:* Like the carved stone font (also built 1420-50), this finely carved and decorated oak pulpit in Ipplepen's fourteenth-century parish church is most attractive. Its medieval colours have mellowed with age. The base below the pulpit is of a local stone and was put in place during Victorian restoration. In addition to its primary functions, St Andrew's hosts a superb annual flower festival. The postcard was postally used in April 1911.

*Opposite:* The eastern lych gate, off Church Path, leads to the parish church of St Andrew's, Ipplepen. Ipplepen is a large and ancient village (Iplepene in 1086), 8km from Totnes on the road to Newton Abbot. The Perpendicular-style church has a handsome screen with figures in the panelling. The battlemented tower has a full octave peal of bells. Church Path cottages, on the left, are of the same period, and early on were a church house inn. They still have metre-thick walls, exposed beams and open-hearth fireplaces. From the height of the chimney of White Cottage you can tell that these houses were once thatched. The postcard was postally used in 1914. (Chapman & Son, Dawlish)

Stoke Gabriel church. This pretty wooded village is 5km south east of Totnes, and lies at the head of Mill Pool creek on the eastern side of the river Dart. It was a centre of fishing when the river once abounded in salmon. The fifteenth-century parish church of St Gabriel, to the right, is a fine building with a tower containing five bells; it has a massive and ancient yew tree in the churchyard.

*Opposite above:* In the Domesday Book Didasham was the property of the Bishop of Exeter. On the Dart Valley Trail, the little village of Dittisham is seen here through the pines from the Greenway bank of the river Dart. The village is situated at the widest part of the River Dart. At high tide the water stretches for over a mile to Galmpton on the opposite bank. In the past the area was famed for plum growing. Nearby on the Greenway side of the river is land once owned by Sir Walter Ralegh, and the secluded Greenway House where Agatha Christie lived, which is now owned by the National Trust. (Chapman & Son)

*Opposite below:* A hamlet on the bank of the river Dart, near Tuckenhay and Bow Creek, Duncannon is one of the several small communities that can be viewed from the Riverlink steamers that convey passengers between Totnes and Dartmouth during the summer. (Chapman & Son)

Greenway Road, Galmpton. Galmpton (Walementone in 1086) is a small village between Torbay and the river Dart, off the main road between Paignton and Brixham. It has quays and a yacht yard on Galmpton creek, which is a short distance upriver on the opposite bank from Dittisham. (Chapman & Son)

*Opposite above:* A panoramic view, looking north, of Harberton, about 4km south-south-west of Totnes, in a parish which includes six hamlets: Harbertonford, Luscombe, East Leigh, West Leigh, Belsford and Englebourne. The compact village is in a valley reached via a narrow road from the Totnes-Kingsbridge road. The area has good farming land and woodlands, and in the parish, quarries of dunstone (greywacke) and slate were once worked. (E.M. Morison)

*Opposite below:* Alongside the parish church of St Andrew in Harberton is the old Church House Inn, a very popular place among visitors and locals who appreciate real ales and dining on the finest local produce. Originally built for the masons working on the church around 1100, it was later a chantry house with a great hall. Inside there is a fine medieval oak screen, which separates the long bar, with its wood fire at one end, from a most comfortable and welcoming family room. (Nicholas Horne)

*Above:* Harbertonford, on the Totnes to Kingsbridge road, sits on the banks of the small river Harbourn, which in years past frequently flooded lower parts of the village. The largest building in the village was a woollen factory, which later became a corn mill and starch maker. The parish church of St Peter has a rounded apse and a simple interior. Near the entrance porch, there is a obelisk memorial to those who lost their lives in the First World War. Nearby is the Maltsters pub. The pub was previously a brewery, when the main door was wide enough to give access to a horse-drawn dray. Inside, there is a fine collection of old bottles, including some from the local Harbourne Mineral Water Co.

*Opposite above:* Built on a religious site dating from AD 909, Harberton's late medieval parish church of St. Andrew is one of the best examples of the decorated Perpendicular style in Devon. The red, gold and blue decorated fifteenth-century rood screen, the stone pulpit and the mainly Victorian stained-glass windows are dramatic in their brightness. There is a fine Norman red sandstone font. The organ is by Willis of London. The lofty 25m tower has a peal of six bells dating from 1762. The interior reflects the past wealth of the area. Visible in the foreground of this view is the white family vault of Robert and Alida Harvey of Dundridge, built by Messrs Hems & Sons, ecclesiastical sculptors. (W.R. Gay's series)

*Opposite below:* Broadhempston (once called Hempston Magna) is 7km north of Totnes. The interior of the mainly fifteenth-century parish church of St Peter and St Paul includes a plain wooden pulpit and rood screen of the style seen in many of South Devon's smaller country churches restored around 1900. There are a couple of stained-glass windows and a font in stone. The manor anciently belonged to the Canteloupe family, which also held the barony of Totnes at one time, and its lords had the authority to impose capital punishment. The card was postally used in 1913. (W.R. Gay's series)

Loventor Manor, Afton, is mentioned in the Domesday Book as given to Iudhael. The present-day large country house has a much older manor house to the rear, and nearby a cluster of newer buildings is to be found. The manor is near the Gatcombe Brook and is about 6km from Totnes. Access is by a narrow country road from Berry Pomeroy village and Afton. The property, now divided up, has several private owners; the main building was formerly available for functions and receptions. (Jerome Dessain & Co.)

The Rising Sun Inn, Woodland. In the rolling countryside of the valley of the river Dart, between Torbay and Dartmoor, lies this friendly inn. In earlier times this was a drovers' inn. The inn specializes in serving home-made food using local fresh produce, and is famous for its pies. Local real ales and fine wines are available.

*Opposite below:* The interior of the parish church of St David, Ashprington, which was built in the Perpendicular style. An impressive Durant tomb lies on the approach to the church entrance porch. During extensive restoration in 1845-46, the screen doors were removed and are now held by the Exeter City Museum. The door panels, with their four medieval painted figures of saints, were displayed in the Victoria and Albert Museum's Gothic Exhibition in London in October 2003. Disdained by the Victorian restorers, these doors are noted today as good examples of the most common form of West Country Perpendicular tracery. (W.R. Gay's series)

*Above:* A short distance off the Newton Road from Totnes, is the tiny village of Littlehempston (once Hamistona). The parish church of St John the Baptist was rebuilt between 1420 and 1458 and, like many churches, affected by the Victorian enthusiasm for such things, was much restored between 1839 and 1887. The Speechley & Ingram organ was installed in 1868. In the porch is an unusual plaque recording the names of Major Densham (of Buckyett) and the men of the parish who went to the First World War. The belfry has a ring of five bells, two of them medieval.

Ashprington, 4km south east of Totnes, lies near the confluence of the rivers Harbourn and Dart. The land around formed part of the Sharpham Estate, much of which was sold off in the 1940s. Sharpham was held by the Durant family from 1840. On the right of this view is the popular Durant Arms pub run by Graham Ellis. The old building was at one time the Sharpham Estate manager's house. Rising above the village square is the fourteenth-century parish church. The tower has a peal of five bells. (E.M. Morison)

Seen here are stone-built cottages on the upper side of Ashprington's triangular village 'square'. The one shown was formerly a police house, and behind it is a building that was once the village school, up the hill which leads to the parish church gate. (W.R. Gay's series)

Another old cottage in Ashprington, like many others built in local stone. Builders of the few newer homes erected within the village have used the same materials and kept to the traditional style of the much older properties.

# Other Devon titles published by Tempus

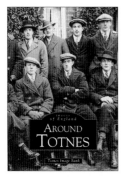

## Around Totnes

TOTNES IMAGE BANK

Tempus' first *Around Totnes* book delves into the history of the south Devon town through a series of evocative and informative images. Recollecting major events such as the fire that destroyed the Civic Hall in 1955, it also captures the everyday through images of Fore Street, St Peter's Quay and the general bustle that surrounds them. Teamed with *Around Totnes in Postcards*, it provides a delicate flavour of this idyllic town.
0 7524 3085 8

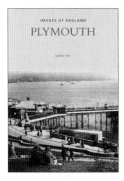

## Plymouth

DEREK TAIT

Rare postcards and photographs illustrate the last century as experienced by Devon's vibrant naval port. Rebuilt from the ashes created by Second World War bombs, Plymouth's history can nevertheless be remembered through this compilation of over 200 archive images. Photographs of buildings, local businesses, theatres and memorabilia of entertainers such as Laurel and Hardy and Harry Houdini provide unique glimpses Plymouth's past.
0 7524 3128 9

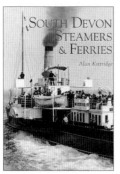

## South Devon Steamers and Ferries

ALAN KITTRIDGE

Holidaymakers travelled in droves to visit the stunning county of Devon and Kittridge's book remembers the subsequent activity of the passenger steamer services. His selection of photographs chosen from his private collection, paint a story of Devon's maritime trade, recall paddle steamer fleets on the Dart and Tamar, Starcross Ferry steamers, and ships such as the *Princess Elizabeth* as she docked into Torquay.
0 7524 2799 7

## Voices of Home Park

JOHN LLOYD

Personal quotes from supporters of Argyle will evoke memories and emotions from Home Park followers. Capturing the essence of victories, defeats, promotions and relegations, epic Cup runs and the variety of events that mark the club's hundred years, this book tells a story through the voices of the many who have witnessed it all. Here, the fans have their say and record this professional club's best and worst moments in their own words.
0 7524 2949 3

If you are interested in purchasing other books published by Tempus, or in case you have difficulty finding any Tempus books in your local bookshop, you can also place orders directly through our website

www.tempus-publishing.com

or from   **BOOKPOST**, Freepost, PO Box 29, Douglas, Isle of Man, IM99 1BQ
tel 01624 836000   email bookshop@enterprise.net